FABER PIANO CO

French Romantic Repertoire

LEVEL 2

Répertoire romantique français

Romantische französische Klavierliteratur

SELECTED AND EDITED BY STEPHEN COOMBS

FABER *ff* MUSIC

CONTENTS

JULES MASSENET   *Papillons blancs*   page 6

DÉODAT DE SÉVERAC   *Stances à Madame de Pompadour*   page 12

ERNEST CHAUSSON   *Sarabande*   page 18

CHARLES GOUNOD   *Matinée de mai*   page 22

GUILLAUME LEKEU   *Fughetta*   page 25

CAMILLE SAINT-SAËNS   *Bagatelle* Op.3 No.3   page 29

JULES MASSENET   *Saltarello* Op.10 No.6   page 32

LILI BOULANGER   *Cortège*   page 36

DÉODAT DE SÉVERAC   *Peppermint-gel*   page 40

This edition © 2001 by Faber Music Ltd
First published in 2001 by Faber Music Ltd
3 Queen Square London WC1N 3AU
Cover picture: *Yvonne and Christine Lerolle Playing the Piano* (1897)
by Pierre-Auguste Renoir
Music processed by MusicSet 2000
French translation by Traduction Faber Music
German translation by Dorothee Göbel
Printed in England by Caligraving Ltd

ISBN 0-571-51958-X

To buy Faber Music publications or to find out about the full range of titles available
please contact your local music retailer or Faber Music sales enquiries:

Faber Music Limited, Burnt Mill, Elizabeth Way, Harlow, CM20 2HX England
Tel: +44 (0)1279 82 89 82   Fax: +44 (0)1279 82 89 83
sales@fabermusic.com   www.fabermusic.com

INTRODUCTION

PARIS in the nineteenth century was the artistic and intellectual centre of Europe. Poets, artists and painters flocked to the capital, creating a diverse cultural flavour and international reputation. A growing number of foreign composers and performers were attracted by its multitude of artistic opportunities, notably Chopin and Liszt, whose profound contribution to piano literature paved the way for successive generations of composers.

It may seem somewhat surprising that French pianism and French piano music should therefore have such a distinctive signature—an elegance and charm that is immediately recognizable. This is largely due to a musical renaissance in France, which began in earnest after the fall of Paris to the Prussians in 1870. In an effort to escape the dominance of foreign culture, the search for a French nationalist voice became paramount.

From concert hall, to theatre, to open-air proms in the Tuileries; the performance possibilities available at this time were endless. The flowering of private societies devoted to the performance of chamber music and the numerous cafés and salons frequented by the bourgeoisie further contributed to the creation of a cultural atmosphere ripe with opportunity. Many of the great pianists of the time lived and worked in Paris, and virtually every pianist of note played there.

Virtuoso composer-performer Friedrich Kalkbrenner was one such performer to take advantage of the heady musical climate. Having studied under Louis Adam at the Paris Conservatoire, he became a central figure in a new generation of piano virtuosos. He developed a technique of rapid, even passage-work based on suppleness and a highly developed finger technique. All the great pianists who graduated from the Paris Conservatoire in the nineteenth century were noted for this style of playing, so it is therefore not surprising that clarity, beauty of tone and fast passage-work became the hallmark of French piano repertoire.

This style was made possible by a series of technical transformations that the piano underwent throughout the nineteenth century, producing what was essentially a new instrument. Subtle nuances of instrumental colour were now possible, as were dramatic changes of dynamic with the instrument's greater capacity for volume.

In literary, artistic and musical circles alike, Romanticism was the avant-garde movement of the day. In all its guises, the Romantic spirit had the nervous sensations and emotional impulses of the individual at its heart. However, from 1870, French composers explored a new form of Romanticism. Adopting the motto 'Ars Gallica', they concentrated on the form, colour and texture of sound. This meant that French music began to be descriptive rather than emotional; logic, clarity and balance therefore became the ideals of these Romantic composers.

Nowhere were these ideals more clearly demonstrated than in the music of Gounod (1818–1893). Indeed, Saint-Saëns once said of him: 'Expressiveness was always his ideal: that is why there are so few notes in his music ... each note sings ... His aim was to obtain the maximum possible effect with the minimum of apparent effort.'

Camille Saint-Saëns (1835–1921) and Charles Gounod could be described as the two pillars of this 'new' French Romantic music. Saint-Saëns himself was a brilliant pianist and deeply impressed by Liszt's musical genius, although his first two symphonies and piano concerto recall the earlier models of Mozart, Weber and Mendelssohn. Gounod first became known as the composer of the opera *Faust*. He was a friend of the Mendelssohns and spent the years 1842 to 1845 living in Vienna, Berlin and Leipzig. With their knowledge of German culture and music, the figures of Gounod and Saint-Saëns would seem unlikely role models for a nationalistic school of pianism. Yet through their teaching, together they were to influence generations of future composers including the key French figures of Jules Massenet (1842–1912), César Franck (1822–1900) and Déodat de Séverac (1872–1921).

In this collection of French piano music you will find a fascinating world of charm and sophistication, marked by its balance of intellect with emotion. All fingerings and pedal markings are intended as suggestions only. Each piece in this volume has been chosen, primarily, because of the quality of the music and every pianist whether performer, teacher, student or general music lover will find much to delight and surprise them.

STEPHEN COOMBS
April 2001

EINLEITUNG

PARIS war im 19. Jahrhundert künstlerischer und intellektueller Mittelpunkt Europas. Schriftsteller, Künstler und Maler zog es in die französische Hauptstadt, wo ein von kultureller Vielfalt und Internationalität geprägtes Klima entstand. Zunehmend fanden auch ausländische Komponisten und Interpreten den Weg in die Metropole. Sie schätzten vor allem die Vielzahl künstlerischer Wirkungsmöglichkeiten. Zu diesen Künstlern zählten auch Chopin und Liszt, deren wichtige Beiträge zur Klaviermusik den folgenden Komponisten-generationen den Weg ebneten.

Aus diesem Grund mag es überraschen, daß der französische Klavierstil und französische Klaviermusik eine so deutliche eigene Handschrift tragen, daß sie von einer Eleganz und einem Charme geprägt sind, die sich unmittelbar offenbaren. Diese Tatsache ist vor allem auf eine musikalische Erneuerungsbewegung zurückzuführen, die entscheidend mit der Besetzung von Paris durch die Preußen 1870 einsetzte. Die Suche nach einer eigenen französischen Stimme wurde zum dominierenden Faktor bei dem Versuch, die Vorherrschaft einer fremden Kultur abzuschütteln.

Angefangen beim Konzertsaal, über das Theater bis hin zu Freiluftkonzerten in den Tuillerien: die Aufführungs-möglichkeiten dieser Zeit waren unerschöpflich. Die aufblühenden privaten Vereine zur Aufführung von Kammermusik und die zahlreichen, von der Bourgeosie besuchten Cafés und Salons trugen zur Entstehung einer kulturellen Atmosphäre vielfältigster Aufführungs-möglichkeiten bei. Viele der bedeutendsten Pianisten dieser Zeit lebten und arbeiteten in Paris, und wirklich jeder namhafte Pianist musizierte in der französischen Hauptstadt.

Der Klaviervirtuose und Komponist Friedrich Kalkbrenner gehört zu den Interpreten, die sich diese berauschende musikalische Atmosphäre nutzbar machten. Nach seinem Studium bei Louis Adam am Pariser Conservatoire wurde er zu einer zentralen Figur einer neuen Generation von Klaviervirtuosen. Er entwickelte eine Technik schneller, leichter und gleichmässiger Passagen, die auf delikatem Anschlag und einer hochentwickelten Fingertechnik beruhte. Diese Technik beherrschten sämtliche bedeutenden Pianisten, die im neunzehnten Jahrhundert am Pariser Conservatoire studierten, so daß Klarheit, Tonschönheit und schnelles Passagenwerk als zunehmendes Markenzeichen des französischen Klavierrepertoires keineswegs überrascht. Dieser Stil wurde durch eine Reihe technischer Veränderungen im Klavierbau des neunzehnten Jahrhunderts ermöglicht, die praktisch zu einem ganz neuen Instrument führten. Die neue Bauweise des Klavier-instruments ermöglichte zarteste Nuancen instrumentaler Klangfarbe, mit dem Zuwachs an Lautstärke zugleich aber auch dramatische dynamische Schattierungen.

Die Romantik war in literarischen, künstlerischen und musikalischen Kreisen gleichermaßen die Kunstrichtung der Avantgarde. In all seinen verschiedenen Ausprägungen sprach der romantische Geist von den erregten Empfindungen und emotionalen Impulse des einzelnen Individuums. Nach 1870 entwickelten französische Komponisten jedoch eine neue Spielart der Romantik. Unter dem Sigel einer „Ars Gallica" konzentrierten sie sich auf formale Elemente sowie auf Klangfarbe und Klangtextur. Die französische Musik wandelte sich somit zu einer einer eher beschreibenden als emotional empfundenen: Logik, Klarheit und Balance wurden die Ideale dieser romantischen Komponisten.

Nirgends sah man diese Ziele deutlicher verwirklicht als in der Musik von Gounod (1818–1893). Saint-Saëns behauptete einmal von ihm: „Espressivität war immer sein Ziel: deshalb schreibt er so wenige Noten … jede Note singt … sein Ziel war es, mit einem Minimum ersichtlicher Anstrengung ein Maximum möglichen Effekts zu erreichen."

Camille Saint-Saëns (1835–1921) und Charles Gounod könnte man als die beiden führenden Vertreter dieser „neuen" französischen romantischen Musik bezeichnen. Saint-Saëns war ein brillanter Pianist und tief beeindruckt von Liszts musikalischem Genie. Seine ersten beiden Symphonien und das Klavierkonzert erinnern allerdings eher an die früheren Vorbilder von Mozart, Weber und Mendelssohn. Gounod wurde zuerst als Komponist der *Faust* bekannt. Er war mit der Familie Mendelssohn befreundet und lebte während der Jahre 1842–45 in Wien, Berlin und Leipzig. Angesichts ihrer Kenntnis der deutschen Kultur und Musik erscheinen Gounod und Saint-Saëns zunächst als wenig plausible Vertreter einer nationalen französischen Klavierschule. Und doch sollten sie beide durch ihren Unterricht Generationen künftiger Komponisten prägen, darunter so bedeutende französische Komponisten wie Jules Massenet (1842–1912), César Franck (1822–1900) und Déodat de Séverac (1872–1921).

In der vorliegenden Sammlung französischer Klavier-musik findet man eine faszinierende Welt voller Charme und Eleganz, die durch die Balance zwischen Geist und Gefühl geprägt ist. Fingersätze und Hinweise zum Pedal sind lediglich Vorschläge. Jedes einzelne Stück in dieser Sammlung wurde vor allem aufgrund seiner musikalischen Qualität ausgesucht, und jeder Pianist, sei er nun Interpret, Lehrer, Schüler oder ein Musikliebhaber, wird vieles finden, das ihn überraschen und erfreuen wird.

STEPHEN COOMBS
April 2001

INTRODUCTION

AU XIXᵉ SIÈCLE, Paris était le centre intellectuel et artistique de l'Europe. Poètes, artistes et peintres affluaient vers la capitale, asseyant une ambiance culturelle plurielle et une réputation internationale. La multitude des possibilités artistiques offertes par la capitale attira un nombre croissant de compositeurs et d'interprètes étrangers, notamment Chopin et Liszt, dont la profonde contribution à la littérature pianistique ouvrit la voie aux générations de compositeurs suivantes.

Que la pianisme et la musique pianistique français soient marqués d'un tel sceau distinctif—une élégance doublée d'un charme d'emblée reconnaissable—peut dès lors surprendre quelque peu. Ce sceau est un grande partie imputable à la renaissance musicale français, qui commença pour de bon lorsque Paris tomba aux mains des Prussiens, en 1870. Pour échapper à la domination de la culture étrangère, la quête d'une voix nationaliste française se fit primordiale.

Salles de concerts, théâtres, concerts-promenades aux Tuileries: les endroits où jouer, à cette époque, étaient infinis. L'efflorescence de sociétés privées vouées à l'exécution de la musique de chambre, ainsi que les nombreux cafés et salons fréquentés par la bourgeoisie, concoururent également à l'émergence d'une atmosphère culturelle riche en perspectives. Maints grands pianistes de l'époque vécurent et travaillèrent à Paris, où presque tous les pianistes renommés jouèrent.

Le compositeur-interprète virtuose Friedrich Kalkbrenner fut de ces exécutants qui profitèrent de ce climat musical enivrant. Ancien élève de Louis Adam, au Conservatoire de Paris, il devint une figure centrale d'une nouvelle génération de pianistes virtuoses. Il développa un système de passages rapides, unis, fondé sur la souplesse et une technique digitale fort élaborée. Tous les grands pianistes diplômés du Conservatoire de Paris, au XIXᵉ siècle, étaient réputés pour ce style de jeu, aussi n'est-il guère surprenant que le répertoire pianistique français fût marqué au coin de la clarté, de la beauté de ton et des passages rapides. Ce style put voir le jour grâce à une série de transformations techniques subies par le piano au cours du XIXᵉ siècle, pour aboutir à un instrument fondamentalement nouveau. De subtiles nuances de couleur instrumentale furent désormais possibles, à l'instar de spectaculaires changements de dynamique, conséquence d'un accroissement de la capacité de volume de l'instrument.

Dans les cercles littéraires, artistiques et musicaux, le romantisme était le mouvement avant-gardiste du moment. Quel que fût son dehors, l'esprit romantique détenait en son cœur sensations nerveuses et élans émotiennels. Pourtant, à partir de 1870, les compositeurs français explorèrent une nouvelle forme de romantisme. Adoptant la devise «Ars Gallica», ils se concentrèrent sur la forme, la couleur et la texture du son. La musique français commença donc d'être davantage descriptive qu'émotionelle—logique, clarté et équilibre devenant, partent, les idéaux de ces compositeurs romantiques.

Nulle autre musique n'exposa plus clairement ces idéaux que celle de Gounod (1818–1893). Gounod dont Saint-Saëns dit un jour: «L'expressivité fut toujours son idéal: c'est pourquoi sa musique compte si peu de notes … chaque note chante … son but était d'obtenir le maximum d'effets possibles avec le minimum d'efforts apparents.»

Camille Saint-Saëns (1835–1921) et Charles Gounod pourraient être considérés comme les deux piliers de cette «nouvelle» musique romantique français. Lui-même brillant pianiste, Saint-Saëns fut profondément impressionné par le génie musical Lisztien, quoique ses deux premières symphonies et son concerto pour piano soient renouvelés des modèles mozartiens, weberiens et mendelssohniens. Gounod se fit d'abord connaître comme le compositeur le l'opéra *Faust*. Ami de Mendelssohn, il passa les années 1842–45 à Vienne, Berlin et Leipzig. Avec leur connaissance de la culture et de la musique allemandes, Gounod et Saint-Saëns pourraient sembler de bien improbables modèles pour une école de pianisme nationaliste. Pourtant, à travers leur enseignement, ils allaient influencer des générations de compositeurs, parmi lesquels les personnages clés de la musique française que furent Jules Massenet (1842–1912), César Franck (1822–1900) et Déodat de Séverac (1872–1921).

Le présent recueil de musique pianistique française vous fera découvrir un fascinant univers de charme et de sophistication, tout d'équilibre entre intellect et émotion. Tous les doigtés et les indications de pédale se veulent de simples suggestions. Chaque pièce de ce volume a été choisie essentiellement en fonction de la qualité de la musique, et chaque pianiste, qu'il soit interprète, professeur, étudiant ou mélomane, trouvera force matière à ravissement et à surprise.

STEPHEN COOMBS
avril 2001

Papillons blancs

Jules Massenet
(1842–1912)

2 Ped.

Tempo I (Allegro)

Stances à Madame de Pompadour

Verses for Madame de Pompadour

Déodat de Séverac
(1872–1921)

Lento e molto espressivo

* *Toutes les notes d'ornements doivent être prises sur le temps.* All the ornaments must be played on the beat.
** *Ce point d'orgue ∩ est toujours court.* This pause ∩ is always short.

14

Sarabande

Ernest Chausson
(1855–1899)

Matinée de mai

May Morning

Charles Gounod
(1818–1893)

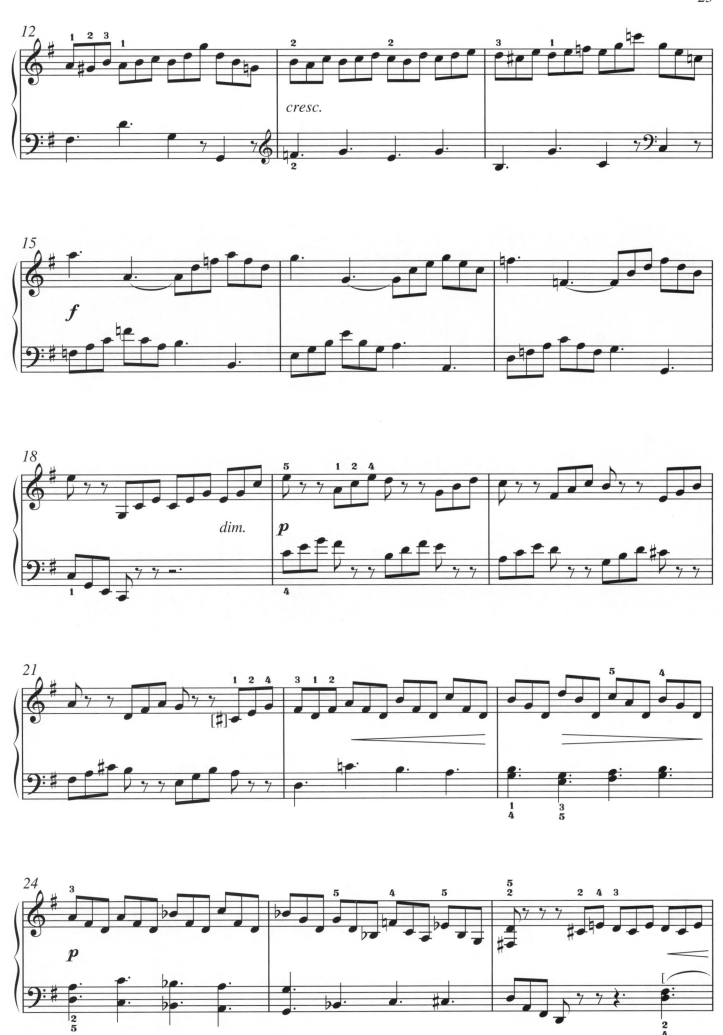

Fughetta

from Sonata for Piano

Guillaume Lekeu
(1870–1894)

Bagatelle

Op.3 No.3

Camille Saint-Saëns
(1835–1921)

Saltarello

Op.10 No.6

Jules Massenet
(1842–1912)

Allegro vivace ♩. = 160

il basso marcato e staccato

à Yvonne Astruc

Cortège
Procession

Lili Boulanger
(1893–1918)

* performing suggestion

Au cher GODCIPAC Toulousain d'Honneur

Peppermint-gel

Valse brillante de concert

Déodat de Séverac
(1872–1921)

Dans un mouvement assez vif

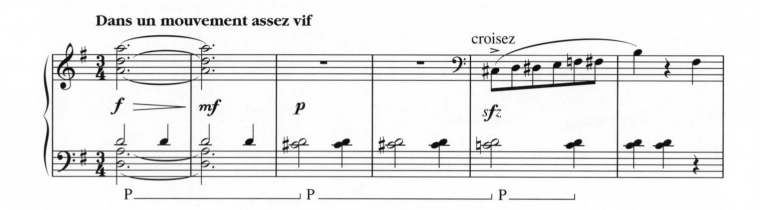

Vif quasi presto

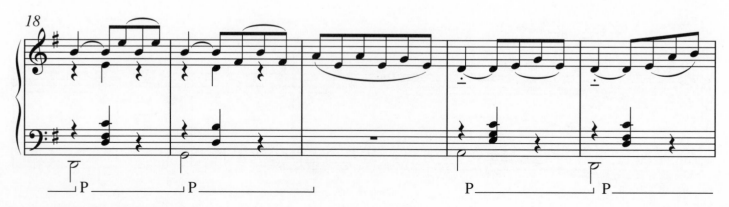